IMAGES OF W

CW00545970

SS TOTENKOPF
AT WAR

A HISTORY OF
THE DIVISION

RARE PHOTOGRAPHS FROM
WARTIME ARCHIVES

Ian Baxter

Pen & Sword
MILITARY

First published in Great Britain in 2017 by
PEN & SWORD MILITARY
An imprint of
Pen & Sword Books Ltd
47 Church Street
Barnsley
South Yorkshire
S70 2AS

Copyright © Ian Baxter, 2017

ISBN 978-1-47389-093-0

The right of Ian Baxter to be identified as author of this work has been asserted by him in accordance with the Copyright, Designs and Patents Act 1988.

A CIP catalogue record for this book is available from the British Library.

All rights reserved. No part of this book may be reproduced or transmitted in any form or by any means, electronic or mechanical including photocopying, recording or by any information storage and retrieval system, without permission from the Publisher in writing.

Typeset by Concept, Huddersfield, West Yorkshire HD4 5JL.
Printed and bound in England by CPI Group (UK) Ltd, Croydon CR0 4YY.

Pen & Sword Books Ltd incorporates the imprints of Pen & Sword Archaeology, Atlas, Aviation, Battleground, Discovery, Family History, History, Maritime, Military, Naval, Politics, Railways, Select, Social History, Transport, True Crime, and Claymore Press, Frontline Books, Leo Cooper, Praetorian Press, Remember When, Seaforth Publishing and Wharncliffe.

For a complete list of Pen & Sword titles please contact
PEN & SWORD BOOKS LIMITED
47 Church Street, Barnsley, South Yorkshire S70 2AS, England
E-mail: enquiries@pen-and-sword.co.uk
Website: www.pen-and-sword.co.uk

Contents

Introduction

From its organization and training to its fighting on the Western and then the Eastern Front, this book describes the fighting tactics, the uniforms, the battles and the different elements that went into making the infamous Totenkopf (Death's Head) Division into such an effective killing machine. Using 250 previously unpublished and rare photographs, many of which have come from the albums of individuals who took part in the war, the book describes and depicts the great battles the division won and lost. It illustrates key battles such as the attack on France, the invasion of the Soviet Union, the fighting at Kharkov and Kursk, and others.

As the division retreated through the Soviet Union the men of the Totenkopf Division continued to fight to the death. This book tells how the division fought from one part of the front to another, trying in vain to the plug the disintegrating gaps on the smouldering front lines. It describes how this elite band of men fought and murdered its way across Europe and the Soviet Union, and it provides much historical information about the division, the weapons it used, the uniforms it wore, and its battle tactics.

Chapter One

Birth of a Division

Before the Totenkopf achieved divisional status, the formation was known as Kampfgruppe Eicke, commanded by the hard and disciplined SS-Brigadeführer Theodore Eicke. Eicke had been commander of Dachau concentration camp in June 1933 and became a major figure in the SS. He was regarded the architect, builder, and director of the concentration camp system and ruled it with an iron fist. He was stocky in appearance, ruthless, blatantly brutal, and was said to give off an aura of raw energy. Recruits were indoctrinated in SS ideology to believe in the new Aryan order and his men followed his orders with blind and absolute obedience, even if it meant shooting prisoners and committing atrocities against civilians.

From the racially motivated SS-Totenkopfverbände (concentration camp guards) and others members of German militias that had committed a host of terrible crimes, Eicke formed Kampgruppe Eicke in the late 1930s. All recruits were expected to be fit with excellent racial features and produce a certificate of good behavior from the police. They were indoctrinated with a fanatical determination to fight for the Führer, to the death if necessary.

The military training regime took place at the unit's depot at Dachau and was developed by Paul Hausser. He oversaw the military and ideological training with the help of two experienced officers, Cassius Freiherr von Montigny and Felix Steiner.

Hausser was also a hard disciplinarian. His recruits were trained to bury their emotions and become absorbed by their camaraderie and loyalty to the SS.

Recruits spent one week out of every month on guard duty in a concentration camp. At Dachau and other concentration camps they were taught to show hatred for Jews, emigrants, homosexuals and Jehovah's Witnesses. They listened while Eicke or Hausser delivered lectures about the most dangerous enemies of National Socialism. Guard duty often entailed barbaric acts of cruelty on those incarcerated behind the barbed wire fences of the concentration camps. For Eicke, this process weeded out those SS men who were not fit for military duty in the Totenkopf division. They only wanted the most disciplined officers, NCOs, and enlisted men who had absolute allegiance and fanaticism to the SS order. These recruits, now exceptionally efficient killers, became known as the SS-Verfügungstruppe (SS Dispositional Troops) or SS-VT units, Germania and Deutschland.

Through the late 1930s, Totenkopf evolved and expanded considerably. War in September 1939 put strain on the SS-VT to main its levels of manpower. Following the capitulation of Poland in October 1939, Hitler expanded the SS and created three division, the SS Verfügungs Division based around the SS-VT regiments, the Polizei Division created from recruits from the Ordnungspolizei, and Totenkopf. At the same time the Leibstandarte SS Adolf Hitler (Hitler's personal bodyguard) expanded to the size of a motorized regiment. Out of this expansion emerged the military arm of the SS known as the Weapon SS, or Waffen-SS, and the creation a fully-fledged Totenkopf SS-Division. As a result of this formation, Eicke withdrew his staff from Dachau to form and equip his new Totenkopf Division, which was based on a standard Wehrmacht motorized division. It comprised three motorized infantry regiments instead of the regular Wehrmacht divisional establishment of two. The three SS-Totenkopfverbände Standarte formed the basis of the three motorized infantry regiments. For the artillery regiment, SS Heimwehr Danzig were enlisted, and to support the division, SS-Gruppenführer Heinrich Himmler established a replacement battalion for each Totenkopf regiment.

These new recruits of the SS were now a fully established Waffen-SS Division. Since late 1939 some 6,500 men from the SS-VT had been transferred into the new Totenkopf Division. They consisted of the concentration camp guards of the 1st (Oberbayern), 2nd (Brandenburg) and 3rd (Thüringen) Standarten (regiments) of the SS-Totenkopfverbände, and men from the SS Heimwehr Danzig. There were also members of other SS militias that were transferred into the division in early 1940. Some of these units had already shed blood in the Polish campaign and had been involved in numerous massacres against Polish civilians, political leaders and prisoners of war. Now, in May 1940, they were ready to attack the Low Countries and France.

(**Opposite**) SS-Obergruppenführer Theodore Eicke. Eicke had been made commander of Dachau concentration camp in June 1933 and became a major figure in the SS. He was regarded the architect, builder, and director of the concentration camp system and ruled it with an iron fist. On the battlefield he led Totenkopf to a series of victories on the Western Front in 1940, but committed some dreadful crimes against British and North African PoWs. His division went on to become one of the most effective fighting formations in Russia. On 26 February 1943 he was killed during the opening phase of the third battle of Kharkov when his Fieseler Fi 156 Storch aircraft was shot down.

(**Above**) A commanding officer leads his men out of the gates of a training barracks. Every Totenkopf recruit had to be fit, have impeccable racial features, and produce a certificate of good behavior from the police.

(**Opposite**) A photograph showing a commanding officer with his new recruits during a training exercise, late 1930s. The men are armed with the Karabiner 98K bolt action rifle, which was the standard weapon used by the Heer and later the Waffen-SS.

(**Below**) A column of Totenkopf troops on a drill march being led by their commanding officer on horseback. New recruits were indoctrinated with a fanatical determination to fight for the Führer. Men had to blindly obey every order, even if it meant shooting prisoners and committing atrocities against civilians.

(**Above**) Recruits are seen standing near their personal kits and Karabiner 98K bolt action rifles that have been stacked together. They were stacked like this for speedy action.

(**Opposite, above**) Rifle practice in the snow. The recruit is wearing the standard army tunic that remained universal in the Waffen-SS during the war. The commanding officer on the left and his corporal, or Rottenführer, on the right are wearing the army standard greatcoat, which was worn by all ranks of Totenkopf until 1942.

(**Opposite, below**) During peace time and two Totenkopf platoon leaders, or SS-Hauptscharführer, on the right are playing cards with another SS soldier who appears not be part of the Totenkopf. He displays an SS rune on his tunic collar instead of the Totenkopf patch.

(**Above**) Out in the snow in early 1939 and troops are being inspected. The period of enlistment in the original Totenkopf Verbände was initially four years. In 1938 this was increased to twelve years.

(**Opposite**) Training in the snow: a German MG gunner and loader practicing with the Czech made MG ZB-30. The Heer had adopted the ZB-30 after the occupation of Czechoslovakia, renaming it the MG30(t). The weapon was used in a light role. During the early part of the war the Waffen-SS used large numbers of ZB-30s.

A typical SS wardrobe displaying hanging tunics and two pairs of black boots. Aluminum mess tins and other items of kit can also be seen. On top of the wardrobe are two M1935 steel helmets sitting on neatly pressed and folded kit, separated by two corrugated gas mask holders.

A Totenkopf guard. Training of the Totenkopf guards took place at the unit's depot at Dachau. The training for the men was gruelling and the days were long. The Totenkopf were even more brutal than the rest of the armed SS.

Recruits on a training exercise with a Horch cross-country vehicle.

(**Above**) A column of troops belonging to the newly-formed Totenkopf seen on exercise passing over a bridge in Germany. The men are all wearing the standard army issue greatcoat but with SS insignia sewn onto their collar patches. Note to the two young Hitlerjugend boys dressed in black following the march.

(**Opposite**) An honoured guard of Totenkopf follow the first formation of the standard. The Feldzeichen or field banner had an almost religious significance. Each banner was consecrated by the Führer at the Reichsparteitage in Nuremberg – the Nuremberg Rallies – where they touched the Blutfahne, the flag stained with the blood of Nazi 'martyrs' killed during the Munich Beer Hall Putsch of 1923. The flag bearers are seen here in white parade gloves.

(**Below**) A well camouflaged MG34 crew with their trainer during an exercise. The primary gunner (Schütze 1) was usually the most experienced soldier in an MG squad. His team mate (Schütze 2) lying to the left of the gunner, fed the ammunition belts and saw to it that the gun remained operational at all times.

(**Above**) Two photographs taken in sequence showing an SS FlaK gunner demonstrating a 2cm FlaK light anti-aircraft gun in a barracks. The gun's main purpose was to deliver a deadly barrage of explosive shells against enemy aircraft, but they were also fearsome anti-personnel weapons.

(**Opposite, above**) On maneuvers in 1940 Totenkopf machine gun crews during a training exercise. The MG34 most popular and reliable machine gun, used in both light and heavy roles, during the early years of the war.

(**Opposite, below**) Totenkopf pay tribute to a dead comrade. The SS motto '*Meine Ehre Heisst Treue*' (my honour is loyalty) was the foundation of all Waffen-SS actions both in training and bleeding on the battlefield. Every SS man swore an oath to carry out an order issued by the Führer or by a superior, regardless of personal sacrifice.

(**Below**) Photographed inside a barracks at Christmas in 1939, Totenkopf troops are resting. Their rifles can be seen behind them on a wall-mounted rack.

Soldiers pose for a group photograph during training. They are all wearing the standard army greatcoat with the Totenkopf collar patch. Their SS black leather belts carry the carbines for their 98K bolt action rifle. They all wear the M1938 field cap with the 'Death's Head' badge sewn onto the front.

A commanding officer appears to be about to bestow something on one of his men. The rest of the troop appear to have found something amusing and are laughing.

On an exercise is a column of vehicles, mainly support vehicles.

Soldiers are seen cleaning out the Maschinengewehr 08 (MG 08), which was the standard German Army First World War machine gun. It was used for training in the Heer and Waffen-SS and served during the Second War as a heavy machine gun in many German infantry divisions.

New Totenkopf recruits can be seen sitting in a field with their trainer.

Totenkopf troops during a training exercise purposely spaced out across a field on the march. The barracks can be seen in the distance.

Chapter Two

Into Battle
(1940–41)

On 9 May 1940 Hitler finally decided to attack the west. He told his Western Front commanders to signal to all units that they were preparing to attack across the frontiers of Holland, Belgium and Luxembourg and to move to their assembly areas for attack. Later that evening, the codeword 'Danzig' alerted all German forces that they were to attack in the early hours of the next morning.

For the attack against the west, the Wehrmacht were divided into three army groups: A, B and C. The main strike would be given to Army Group A, which would drive its armoured units through the Ardennes, then swing round across the plains of northern France, and then make straight for the Channel coast. By doing this it would cut the Allied force in half and break the main enemy concentration in Belgium between Army Group A advancing from the south and Army Group B in the north. The task of Army Group B was to occupy Holland with motorized forces and to prevent the linking up of the Dutch army with Anglo-Belgian force. It was to destroy the Belgian frontier defences by a rapid and powerful attack and throw the enemy back over the line between Antwerp and Namur. The fortress of Antwerp was to be surrounded from the north and east and the fortress of Liege from the north-east and north of the Meuse.

Army Group C, the most southern of the three, was to engage the garrison of the Maginot Line, penetrating it if possible.

As ground and airborne troops attacked Belgium and Holland during the early hours of 10 May, Totenkopf waited along the border while the SS Verfügungs Division and Leibstandarte were committed to battle.

By the end of the first day, Belgian resistance had been overwhelmed and French forces brushed aside. By the evening of 11 May, German units had reached the Meuse along a 100-mile front, from Sedan to Dinant. They had advanced nearly ninety miles in three days. The demoralized French Army withdrew in confusion to Antwerp along roads clogged with refugees. To the south, French troops immobilized in the Maginot Line were unable to intervene against strong German forces and could not move for lack of transport.

The Belgian Army, having suffered appalling casualties, were streaming back in their thousands to the British Expeditionary Forces (BEF) defence line. Much of the Belgian artillery was pulled by horses or mules, and the wounded were carried on carts. It was a defeated army trying desperately to escape slaughter.

Elsewhere along the front lines the situation was equally grim. Dutch troops had tried to hold their meagre positions against overwhelming forces but were swiftly battered into submission by German Blitzkrieg tactics.

A week later, Totenkopf, which was one of the few motorized formations in reserve, was finally released to join the armoured spearhead of Army Group A. The division was ordered to strike across southern Holland, through Belgium into France, and link up with General Hoth's 15th Panzer Corps.

During Totenkopf's march westward they encountered no resistance whatsoever, only becoming entangled in massive traffic jams to the rear of Army Group B. However on 19 May they were ordered to engage the enemy and follow the 15th Panzer Corps drive into France towards the village of Le Cateaux, where Rommel's 7th Panzer Division was embroiled in heavy enemy contact. Here the 1st Infantry Regiment, commanded by Standartenführer Max Simon, with heavy anti-tank, engineer and artillery companies, were moved in to support Rommel. Along the front Totenkopf troops crossed the Sambre River and drove at speed towards Cambrai and La Cateaux, soon encountering resistance from French Moroccan troops. Following several intense engagements, some of which were house-to house battles, the Moroccans were finally ground down. Cambrai was taken with 16,000 prisoners and much battlefield booty. The victory by the Totenkopf allowed Hoth to continue his drive unhampered.

By nightfall of 22 May it was reported that Guderian's 2nd Panzer Division, after a drive of 40 miles, had reached the outskirts of Boulogne.

Further up the coast, in the battered town of Calais, the situation of the BEF was dire. As disaster loomed in France for the Anglo-French armies it was becoming clear to the British that their hopes would rest entirely on the port of Dunkirk and its beaches, where they hoped to be evacuated back to the shores of southern England.

In spite of the seriousness of the military situation, British forces still put up fierce resistance and caused the Totenkopf considerable casualties. The British attack, though poorly planned and with no proper support, so surprised the Totenkopf that their advance was temporarily halted. Eicke was compelled to bring up the division's artillery against advancing British tanks and finally German aerial attacks blunted this assault.

Once they had attended to their men and equipment, Totenkopf resumed its drive towards the town of Bethune on the La Bassée canal. Again, the SS were forced to withdraw from the town due to fierce British resistance. Undeterred, the 3rd SS Infantry Regiment, personally led by Eicke, forced a crossing lower down the canal and successfully established a bridgehead. However, on 24 May Eicke received a 'Führer Order': 'To halt commencement of operations'. This held Army Group A's armour along the canal and prevented any further attacks. Eicke, along with other divisional commanders, was amazed at the halt order, and angry that now they were prevented from crushing the British, allowing them to escape towards Dunkirk.

Two days later, on 26 May, the halt order was rescinded. The 3rd SS Infantry Regiment resumed its attack across the canal and secured a foothold, under heavy British bombardment. A pontoon was hastily erected across the canal and a general advance was ordered to take Bethune. The contact that followed, against the British 2nd Division, was the fiercest enemy contact that Totenkopf had endured so far. Totenkopf troops found the quality of their opposition uneven – at one moment a handful of them were receiving wholesale enemy surrenders, at the next, an entire regiment were being held up by stubborn resistance of a company of British troops with a detachment of artillery and anti-tank guns. Their frustration, coupled with their hatred of the enemy, had led to the murder of ninety-seven men of the prisoners from the Royal Norfolk Regiment.

Following the massacre, heavy fighting continued against the British as they withdrew towards Dunkirk. Once British troops had escaped behind the relative safety of the Dunkirk perimeter the Totenkopf were ordered to halt. This completed the division's part in the first phase of the battle for France.

Next Totenkopf was briefly pulled out of the line and sent to an area around Boulogne for occupational duties, and then on 14 June it was ordered to push southwards to participate in the final defeat of the French Army, where it clashed near Dijon, again with Moroccan troops. All captured Moroccan troops were murdered. In the eyes of the SS, they were sub-human.

Unperturbed, Totenkopf continued its drive south, mopping up the last remnants of the French Army. When France finally capitulated on 22 June, Totenkopf was pulled out of line and assigned to occupational duties near the Spanish border.

The French campaign had proved that Totenkopf could perform as well as the Leibstandarte and Das Reich on the battlefield. It had been resilient and skillful in its deployments, sometimes against enemy units far greater in strength than its own.

Following the victory over the West, Totenkopf strengthened its firepower. Motorized infantry regiments were converted into battle-groups or Kampfgruppen, and additional FlaK and heavy artillery was added.

In late 1940 and early 1941, while Totenkopf continued to train hard in France, preparations were being made by Hitler for the invasion of the Soviet Union, known later as Operation Barbarossa. In April 1941 Totenkopf was instructed that it would move east. In early May all leave was cancelled and the division was made ready to move by rail. On 3 June, main elements of the division were transported from

Bordeaux to East Prussia in sealed cars. After debarkation Totenkopf was positioned along the Lithuanian border in preparation.

For the invasion the division was attached to Hoepner's 4th Panzer Group, which was part of Army Group North. However, Hoepner and Eicke had a dislike for each other, and as a result Totenkopf was put in reserve for the second time in its operational history.

Throughout June along the frontier with Russia, the German Army assembled some three million men, divided into 105 infantry divisions and 32 Panzer divisions. There were 3,332 tanks, over 7,000 artillery pieces, 60,000 motor vehicles and 625,000 horses. This massive force was distributed into three German Army Groups:

- Army Group North, commanded by General Wilhelm Ritter von Leeb: He had assembled his forces in East Prussia on the Lithuanian frontier and his force provided the main spearhead for the advance on Leningrad.
- Army Group Centre, commanded by General Fedor von Bock: This assembled on the 1939 Polish/Russian Frontier, both north and south of Warsaw, and consisted of forty-two infantry divisions of the 4th and 9th Armies and Panzergroups II and III. This army contained the largest number of German infantry and Panzer divisions in all three army groups.
- Army Group South, commanded by Feldmarshal von Runstedt.

During the early morning of 22 June 1941 Barbarossa went into action. The infantry and panzer divisions soon smashed through the bewildered Russian forces on every front. Some of the Red Army forces they surrounded were gigantic. Groups of up to fifteen Russian divisions were trapped at a time.

On the northern front, Leeb's Army Group North was given the task of destroying the Red Army fighting in the Baltic region. It was to thrust across East Prussia, liquidating the bases of the Baltic Fleet, destroying what was left of Russian naval power and capturing Kronstadt and Leningrad. Once Leningrad had been taken, the German armies could sweep down from the north while the main force closed in from the west. With half a million men at Leeb's disposal, comprising almost thirty divisions, six of them armoured and motorized with 1,500 Panzers and 12,000 heavy weapons, plus an air fleet of nearly 1,000 planes, he was determined to dispose of the Russian force once and for all.

Leeb's two-pronged offensive along the Baltic opened up at first light on the morning of 22 June. His force, consisting of 16th and 18th armies, smashed through the Soviet defences. Russian soldiers stood helpless in its path, too shocked to act. Over the weeks to come, German troops of Army Group North continued to chew their way through enemy positions, through Lithuania, Latvia and Estonia, towards their objective – Leningrad. The earth was baked by the summer heat and Leeb's army was able to advance rapidly through the Baltic states.

Within two days of the invasion, Totenkopf crossed the border, cleared the Lithuanian forests around Jurbarkas and then swept through towards the Dvina. Once there, Totenkopf was assigned to Manstein's 56th Panzer Corps and given the task of defending the corp's flank and maintaining contact with the 16th Army to the south.

By July Totenkopf was embroiled in heavy fighting along the Stalin line. This became a fierce contest of attrition, and although the Russians showed fortitude and determination, they were constantly hampered by lack of weapons and manpower. The remaining troops holding out along the line were subjected to merciless ground and aerial bombardments and by mid-July the line was breached.

At the rate Army Group were advancing, they would need no more than nine or ten days to reach the outskirts of Leningrad, but following their surge of success, the German army and soldiers of the Totenkopf were losing momentum. Not only were their supply lines being overstretched, but enemy resistance began to stiffen. These Russian soldiers were now the sole barrier between Leningrad and the Germans. The last bastion of defence in front of the imperial city was Lake Ilmen.

By 21 August the defence of Lake Ilmen was finally overcome with eight Soviet divisions being destroyed. Totenkopf captured more prisoners in one day than they had done in the entire French campaign. Yet, for all the success, the Russian position was stronger. While German forces had been making good progress, troops were still entangled in hundreds of miles of earth walls, anti-tank ditches, wire barricades, thousands of defensive pillboxes, and the harrying activities of Russian tanks on the road east. Every mile the Germans moved, they came up against stiffening resistance.

In the Demyansk area in mid-September heavy fighting wore down Totenkopf units to the point where they reluctantly had to dig in and await assistance.

Fighting continued, and at Lushno Soviet forces overran Totenkopf positions, which they managed to stabilize only with fanatical resilience and courage. Action continued with unabated ferocity. Lushno changed hands four times, but on 27 September the men of the SS finally captured the village.

While Lushno was a victory, it was a defensive victory. The Totenkopf had fought for their lives in the swamps, lakes and forest. They had underestimated their Red foe and the terrain in which they were operating. The vastness of the countryside together with the intensity with which the Russians were fighting amounted to a war completely different from that which they had experienced in the West a year earlier. As September drew to a close, a newer more deadlier threat loomed, a Russian winter.

Before operations against the west in 1940, and men belonging to a field kitchen unit can be seen with an HF 12 small kitchen wagon. These wagons could operate on the move, cooking stews, soups, and coffee, the limber carried utensils and equipment. The troops nicknamed them 'goulash cannons'. Note the Totenkopf symbol painted on the wagon's mudguard.

Two commanding officers confer on a road during the opening phase of the attack against the west. The officers are part of the SS Panzergrenadier Regiment 6 'Theodor Eicke'. During the campaign in France, Totenkopf served initially as a part of the Army reserve. On 16 May 1940, the division was ordered into battle, and on the 19th it was ordered to secure the area of Le Cateau and Cambrai.

An SS-Obersturmführer (SS-senior assault leader) is seen handing out something to his men from the back of a support vehicle during the campaign on the Western Front in 1940.

A photograph showing a pontoon bridge erected across a river. First, engineers would position the pontoon boats (either inflatable or 50-foot pontoon boats), and then the bridging equipment would be erected across it – in a surprisingly short time. Some of the pontoon boats were fitted with outboard motors to hold the sections in place against the often strong currents. There were so many waterways that needed to be crossed by so many different divisions that the Germans found they were running out of bridging equipment.

(**Opposite, above**) An infantry truck carrying Totenkopf troops is seen moving towards the front. Foliage has been applied to the vehicle to help conceal it from the air. Rolled netting can also be seen, which was used when the vehicle was stationary for any length of time. Note the national flag draped over the engine deck for aerial recognition.

(**Opposite, below**) Totenkopf vehicles move along a road during the division's drive. SS infantry can be seen in the field next to an abandoned French Renault R-35 light tank. Of the 3,132 modern tanks available to the French forces in May 1940, some 900 were Renault R-35s.

(**Above**) Passing destroyed vehicles of the French Army, Totenkopf soldiers move north and east of Cambrai. Although the Totenkopf had incurred its first wartime combat losses, with 16 dead and 53 wounded, it had relieved the pressure on Rommel's 7th Panzer Division and allowed Hoth's 15th Panzer Corps to continue its drive through France.

Vehicles belonging to a Totenkopf regiment have halted inside a French town. By the look of the faces on the troops they are in an ebullient mood. Congestion along French roads was a constant hindrance to German operations.

Totenkopf troops from the side of the road watch the endless stream of fleeing refugees pouring westward through France. One of the biggest problems for the German drive on the Western Front was the vast number of refugees jamming the already congested road network. British and French forces experienced the same problem, with the added complication of being subjected to constant ground and aerial attacks as they withdrew ahead of the rapidly advancing German armoured spearheads.

Holding a pair of 6 × 8 Zeiss binoculars a troop leader leads a light MG34 machine gun squad forward. In German the term light defined the role and not the weight of the gun. The MG34 had tremendous staying power against enemy infantry, and troops deployed their machine guns for long periods in the most advantageous defensive and offensive positions they could find.

(**Opposite, above**) A group of Totenkopf troops pose for the camera around an SS motorcycle combination in the Arras sector. It was in this area on 21 May 1940 that the Totenkopf Division sustained a heavy mauling by British and French forces.

(**Opposite, below**) During operations on the Western Front and a heavy 7.92cm MG34 squad can be seen cleaning their weapon during a lull in the fighting. This heavy MG34 has been dismounted from the Lafette 34 tripod. Note the pads on the front of the tripod which allowed the MG carrier to sling the weapon over his shoulder with the pads resting on his back.

(**Above**) German vehicles inside a ruined French town in May 1940. They belong to the 7th Panzer Division, which was one of the most successful divisions in the Western Front campaign and covered vast distances in short periods of time. Rommel's Panzer force soon earned the name of the Gespensterdivision (phantom division) because of its speed and the fact that not even the German High Command knew exactly where it was on the situation maps. It was the 7th Panzer Division that was flanked by the Totenkopf on 20 May near Arras.

A Totenkopf unit inside a destroyed French village in May 1940. A motorcyclist can be seen consulting his map. During this early period of the war motorcyclists still rode into battle and dismounted to fight. However they soon began to realize how vulnerable their riders were to small-arms fire and booby traps.

Totenkopf troops march past the carnage wrought to a French column as it retreated across France. Dead horses littered along the road is a grim reminder of what the BEF were compelled to endure.

Troops relax in front of a First World War monument during a lull in the fighting. The battle of France was the kind of fighting that every SS soldier liked best, demanding improvisation, daring and speed.

Two NCOs consult a map near Arras. It was at Arras that the Totenkopf was overrun, finding their standard anti-tank 3.7cm PaK 36 guns were no match for the British Matilda tank. The advance guard of Totenkopf suffered heavy casualties. They limped on to Warlus where German tanks counter-attacked Warlus and Duisans. What ensued was further heavy fighting with Totenkopf repulsing several attacks. Eventually the British were successfully driven back, but they had stalled the German advance, much to the anger of the Totenkopf.

Four photographs showing the 1st Totenkopf Infantry Regiment with a handful of captured Moroccan soldiers in the Cambrai region of France. By the end of the morning of 20 May 1940, Totenkopf units cleared the areas north and east of Cambrai and captured some 16,000 prisoners, of which 200 were Moroccan, and a large amount of battlefield booty. It is uncertain how many of the Moroccans were executed, but certainly most were killed by racially motivated Totenkopf troops.

(**Opposite, above**) When the war in France was over, Totenkopf were ordered to Bordeaux to prepare to occupy the coastal sector. It was in this region that the division's units recouped, recruited and trained. In this photograph an SS-Oberscharführer (SS-Senior platoon leader) can be seen with his men training in southern France.

(**Opposite, below**) Prior to operations in Russia in June 1941, a group of Scharführer of the SS Panzergrenadier Regiment 6 'Theodor Eicke' are conferring around a table.

(**Above**) Officers of 'Theodor Eicke' discuss operations during the initial stages of the attack into Russia. The officer with the Zeiss binoculars around his neck holds the rank of SS-Obersturmführer.

Totenkopf troops during the initial stages of its attack through Russia in late June 1941. The invasion began on 22 June and within two days Totenkopf crossed the border and cleared the Lithunanian forests around Jurbarkas and then swept through towards Dvina. Once there Totenkopf was assigned to Manstein's 56th Panzer Corps.

On the Eastern Front in the summer of 1941, and troops can be seen deploying a searchlight on the battlefield. During the early part of the war in Russia the Germans deployed early war tactics by moving searchlights forward of the FlaK guns in a grid covering an area of about 3 miles between each light. Later in the war searchlights were replaced by radar systems for searching ground targets.

The grave of SS Mann Hermann Hitschler killed in action in Russia on 10 July 1941.

Vehicles have pulled into a small village during the early stages of the campaign in Russia. Note the soldier wearing the 'Type I plain tree summer camouflage tunic' (1936–42). It was worn over the field equipment and had a low waist band with vertical slits above it for easy access to the equipment.

A support vehicle crossing a shallow river in Russia in July 1941. The soldier wearing the Type I plain tree summer camouflage tunic is directing the traffic.

A Totenkopf 5cm PaK 38 crew pose for the camera. Much of the German arsenal in 1941 was towed by animals.

Troops watch a mechanic attending to a support vehicle that has developed a problem. Distances through Russia were vast and breakdowns were frequent.

A FlaK crew with their 2cm gun on tow pose for the camera. These weapons could be fired either on their trailer or when ground mounted. They were used extensively by the Luftwaffe, Heer, Waffen-SS, and Navy. FlaK was divided into three categories based on their calibre: light, 12.7–2cm; medium, 3.7–5cm; and heavy, 8cm and larger.

Every infantry battalion fielded eight MG34 heavy machine guns on the sustained-fire mount, which in 1941 was regarded as more than enough to keep open the flanks for attacking infantry. In this photograph a heavy MG Totenkopf squad are in action with their MG34 mounted on the Lafette 34 stand.

Two photographs showing a 2cm FlaK gun. Although these light anti-aircraft guns were used extensively to deal with the Soviet Air Force, the recurring appearance of heavier enemy armour compelled many FlaK crews to divert their attention from the air and support their own infantry and armour on the ground in an anti-tank role.

(**Opposite, above**) A FlaK gun position in the summer of 1941. Note one of the crew members with an optical range finder which was used to correct fire for the battery. Should rounds fall short or over the target, his task was to advise the aimer on the corrections needed to hit the target.

(**Opposite, below**) A Totenkopf despatch rider on a Wehrmacht registered motorcycle. All motorcycle units and individual motorcyclists, regardless of rank, were issued with the loose-fitting, rubberized coat. The tail of the coat could be gathered in around the wearer's legs and buttoned in position.

(**Above**) A well concealed and well positioned MG34 machine gunner was quite capable of holding up large numbers of attacking infantry. In fact, just a couple of well-sited adequately-supplied machine guns could hold up an entire attacking unit on a frontage of 5 miles or more.

(**Above**) An MG34 crew in action with their MG34 Lafette. An important feature of this weapon was that the legs could be extended to allow it to be used in the anti-aircraft role. When lowered, it could be placed to allow the gun to be fired remotely, or aimed through a periscope attached to the tripod. It was a successful gun and used extensively until the end of the war. In defensive positions, which became more familiar after mid-1943, the MG34 Lafette could hold up entire enemy units for hours or even days. The Russians approached them with caution.

(**Opposite, above**) A heavy MG34 machine gun crew. The gun is mounted on the Lafatte 34 tripod complete with optical site. It could fire 900 rounds per minute – very rapid compared to most enemy machine guns.

(**Opposite, below**) A StuG.III manoeuvres along a road in a town, supporting two Totenkopf troops. During the early phase of the invasion of the Soviet Union the StuG proved its worth, especially when clearing out enemy infantry in urban areas. However, because of its fixed turret it was limited. The vehicle kept pace with the infantry and supported them in almost all types of engagement.

(**Opposite, above**) Maintenance personnel during a break. Vehicles were constantly developing mechanical problems, and it was these men that helped keep the units moving. Much was owed to the maintenance teams.

(**Opposite, below**) Infantry try to moved stranded support vehicles along a muddy road. The mud in Russia was disastrous for mobility. A downpour could bring a whole column to a halt.

(**Above**) The first of two photographs taken in sequence showing captured Russian soldiers, including female personnel. Once German forces had occupied an area, various administrative personnel were moved into the newly occupied zone, such as military policemen – *Feldgendarmerie*. A Totenkopf soldier can be seen acting as a Feldgendarme. This is indicated by the dull aluminum gorget plate suspended around his neck by a chain.

An infantryman in late 1941 during arctic conditions on the Eastern Front. In order to help combat freezing temperatures the soldier has wrapped a scarf around the lower half of his face. Often the soldiers wore a toque – a sleeve-like wool tube that was designed to be pulled over the head to protect the wearer's neck and parts of the face from the bitter cold. Occasionally two or even three toques were worn for extra insulation, along with scarves.

(**Opposite, above**) The second of two photographs taken in sequence showing captured Russian soldiers

(**Opposite, below**) Because of the large numbers of rivers and streams encountered during the advance, all kinds of bridging and river crossing equipment were essential if the Germans were to successfully achieve their objectives. In this photograph Totenkopf are erecting bridging sections.

(**Above**) In the snow and a PaK 35/36 anti-tank crew can be seen defending a road. Even though by 1941 these guns were regarded as inadequate against Soviet armour, they were still quite capable of causing serious damage to their opponent.

(**Opposite, above**) A partly camouflaged 3.7cm PaK 35/36 anti-tank gun. The gun was carried on a two-wheel split-trail carriage of tubular construction with a small sloped splinter shield. This gun emerged as the first anti-tank weapon to serve both the Heer and Waffen-SS.

(**Opposite, below**) During the first half of the war, 2cm FlaK guns were used in all parts of the front to deal with the regenerated threat of the Soviet Air Force.

(**Above**) Regular and Waffen-SS troops are seen queuing to be served their rations from an HF12 field kitchen wagon on a flatbed railway car. During the drive east in 1941, rations were generally good, but frequently these field kitchens were unable to keep pace with the rapid of advance of the troops. As a consequence, soldiers were compelled to improvise the best they could.

(**Opposite, above**) A FlaK crew can be seen with their 2cm gun mounted on a halftrack.

(**Opposite, below**) Three soldiers belonging to SS Panzergrenadier Regiment 6 'Theodor Eicke' stand in front of the entrance of their shelter during winter operations on the Eastern Front in late 1941. Many of these bunker shelters were built along the front.

Here a guard can be seen wearing an animal skin greatcoat over his army field service uniform. This greatcoat was effective for keeping warm, but its light colour meant that it could quickly become soiled with dirt.

In the snow on the Eastern Front and a mortar crew can be seen preparing their Granatwerfer 42 sGW 42 mortar. This deadly weapon was developed in direct response to encounters with the heavy Russian mortar of the same calibre; the Germans designed a virtual copy of the Red Army weapon.

Chapter Three

Bitter Fighting (1941–44)

By October 1941, Totenkopf had been weakened by its defensive action. The division had suffered some 6,600 casualties with only 2,500 replacements since the invasion had started. The division was still ordered to advance East, even though it could only really perform defensive fighting. East of Lushno the units were once again embroiled in heavy fighting and halted against repeated strong Soviet resistance. To add to the problems on the battlefield cold driving rain fell on the front and within hours the Russian countryside had been turned into a quagmire with roads and fields becoming virtually impassable. Although tanks and other tracked vehicles managed to push through the mire at slow pace, animal draft, trucks and other wheeled vehicles became hopelessly stuck. To make matters worse, German supply lines were becoming increasingly overstretched, their vehicles were breaking down, and casualty returns were mounting. When the snow arrived, the front had stagnated and Totenkopf troops dug in for the winter. The Russians, as predicted, finally ran out of power because of the harsh weather, and were unable to achieve any penetration into the German lines – this saved the front from destruction.

Following the traumatic winter of 1941, the German leadership were determined that 1942 would bring a successful outcome to the campaign in the Soviet Union. Yet, the New Year opened with the German army struggling for survival. The 'Das Reich' Division for instance, which had fought in front of Moscow, had lost more than half of its fighting strength. Further north on the Leningrad Front, the Totenkopf Division had fared not much better and were embroiled in heavy fighting, again in the region of Demyansk.

By early February 1942, some 95,000 German troops had become trapped in the 'Demyansk Pocket'. Throughout March, fighting continued to rage with German troops trying in vain to escape the pocket. It was not until April that a bridgehead was finally established between the soldiers in the pocket and the rest of Army Group North. The survival of the Totenkopf trapped inside the pocket was a great achievement and contributed significantly to the stabilization of the German position around Lake Ilmen.

Through the rest of the year they were to continue to wage a battle of attrition against their irrepressible foe, and even began to respect their determination and tenacity. Yet in spite winning a number of successful battles against the Red Army it soon became apparent to the German leadership that there would be no victory that year.

By early 1943, the SS divisions on the Eastern Front had been numbered and some had been upgraded to full Panzer status. The Waffen-SS represented around five percent of the fighting strength of the German forces and more than a quarter of all its Panzer forces. The 'classic' SS divisions – Leibstandarte, Das Reich, Totenkopf, Polizei, Wiking and Nord – had all played their part in the war on the Eastern Front and were now overstretched. To alleviate its manpower shortages the Waffen-SS recruited foreign soldiers into newly created Waffen-SS divisions.

In February 1943 the Soviets were intoxicated by their victory at Stalingrad and Hitler was resolute not to allow Kharkov to fall into enemy hands. The task of carrying out the battle for Kharkov was given to SS-Obergruppenführer Paul 'Papa' Hausser's newly created II SS-Panzer-Korps. Hausser's SS-Korps was ordered to fight to the death inside the rubble strewn city, but after days of continuous combat were compelled to evacuate it, much to the anger of Hitler.

On 4 March, determined to retake Kharkov, the 4th Panzer Army joined forces with the II SS-Panzer-Korps and 'Das Reich' and launched a massive attack penetrating the outskirts of the city. To the north the Leibstandarte's Panzer Regiments I and II smashed their way into Kharkov. Fierce fighting ensued and as Soviet forces escaped onto the Kharkov–Belgorod road, Totenkopf troops were there ready to annihilate them.

The victory at Kharkov was now complete. The victory had come with a heavy price in blood, with some 12,000 soldiers killed, but with the city retaken, Hitler now confidently planned a new offensive against the Kursk salient. Here Hitler was confronted with a tempting strategic opportunity that would, he predicted, deliver him victory.

On 5 July 1943, the II SS-Panzer-Korps, which comprised the 'Leibstandarte', 'Das Reich' and 'Totenkopf' Divisions, attacked in the pre-dawn light along the Kursk salient. The task of the SS-Panzer-Korps was to advance via Beresov and Sadeynoye and smash through the first defensive belt. After this was achieved the next objective was to break through the second line of Russian positions between Lutchki and Jakovlevo. Once these were destroyed the advance would follow in a north-easterly direction. For this operation the 167 Infanterie-Division would form part of the SS Korps and would guard the left flank.

The soldiers of the Totenkopf division wasted no time and smashed a series of strong Soviet defence lines. Das Reich also made progress and by evening of the first day Totenkopf, Leibstandarte and Das Reich had in some places penetrated 13 miles into the Russian defences. Over the next few days the advance continued to go well with Totenkopf smashing its way through more than 30 miles of Russian line, while Leibstandarte and Das Reich were equally successful, despite heavy casualties.

On 9 July, the SS-Panzer-Korps continued heavy fighting against strong enemy forces. Although in danger of being cut off and encircled, they pushed forward and attacked Soviet troops northeast of Beregovoy. During the advance, Das Reich guarded the eastern flank of Totenkopf and Leibstandarte. En route on 12 July it became embroiled in bitter fighting in a huge tank battle in the hills around Prokhorovka. Here the Soviet 5th Guard and 5th Guard Tank Armies clashed with the powerful armoured SS units which was the climax of Operation Zitadelle.

During the showdown the SS remained on the defensive, repelling a number of armoured and infantry attacks. Less than a week after the start of Zitadelle, both sides had lost several hundred tanks and thousands of troops. Although Russian losses in both men and equipment far exceeded the German, their losses could be replaced. German losses, except where armour could be recovered, were not replaceable. The SS divisions, Leibstandarte, Das Reich and Totenkopf, had lost more than half their vehicles and taken massive casualties. The Red Army had suffered much higher losses with some 177,000 being killed and injured, and a staggering 2,586 tanks and self-propelled guns lost during the battle.

By 13 July, the II SS-Panzer-Korps was unable to make any further progress, and poor ground conditions were hampering its logistics. Despite efforts to batter their way through, SS troops had neither the strength nor resources to do so. The cream of the German Panzer force, so carefully concentrated before the operation, was exhausted and the Russians had gained the initiative in the east. The campaign in Russia would now consist of a series of German withdrawals, with the Waffen-SS contesting every inch of the way.

In the southern sector of the Eastern Front, German troops frantically withdrew as Russian forces smashed through the Mius defences and advanced at speed towards Stalino and Taganrog, along the northern coast of the Sea of Azov. Although SS troops of Das Reich and Totenkopf distinguished themselves with their bravery, they could only manage to stem the Red Army for short periods of time.

By mid-August 1943, the Russians had wrenched open a huge gap in the German lines west of Kursk, once again threatening to retake the important industrial city of Kharkov. Das Reich, Totenkopf and Wiking divisions were thrown into battle to prevent the loss of the city. Although all these combat formations were weakened by the Zitadelle disaster, they were still a formidable fighting force. The city had only been recaptured by the Waffen-SS in March 1943, and now it was the Red Army's turn to launch a pincer attack to capture it back again.

Within days of the SS redeployment to Kharkov the Russian 53rd Army driving from north and the 57th Army advancing from the south attacked the city in strength.

Over the next few days the SS scored some outstanding successes in localized combats with Russian armoured units, but, with acute shortages in men and equipment the situation deteriorated by the day.

By early September Hitler grudgingly decided to allow troops to pull out of the doomed city. By early September, with ever increasing losses in men and material, Kharkov was finally evacuated and the SS undertook a spirited withdrawal towards the River Dnieper. Here they managed to halt the Russian onslaught towards the river, allowing Manstein's forces to retreat and redeploy.

Throughout the weeks that followed, German front lines were pulled farther westwards with SS units defending, attacking and counter-attacking as the situation demanded. Their new role as the so-called 'fire brigades', being shuttled from one danger spot to another to face down Russian attacks, typified their position during late 1943.

By early January 1944 the situation on the Eastern Front for the SS had deteriorated in spite its distinguished performance. The Totenkopf were tasked with defending the Dnieper near Krivoi Rog. Fighting along the river was remorseless and losses were high. During their defence the division found itself embroiled in the relief of German troops in what became known as the Korsun Pocket.

Along the German front, Totenkopf troops were experiencing problems in many areas and in spite of strongly held positions, which were manned with an assortment of Pak guns and lines of machine gun pits, the Red Army moved forward in their hundreds regardless of the cost in life, squeezing the pocket. All along the battered front, SS troops tried in vain to hold their positions against overwhelming odds.

In the second week of March, following a ferocious battle near Kirovograd, Totenkopf troops reluctantly fell back behind the Bug. Here they continued their defence. Already the Russian advance in the south had brought its armies perilously close to the borders of Hungary. Before panic had spread across the southern front, Hitler had ordered Operation Margarethe – the German occupation of Hungary. The operation largely involved Waffen-SS and second-rate SS combat formations being used as 'fire brigade' units. By April 1944, the 16 SS-Panzergrenadier-Division 'Reichsführer-SS', the 18 SS-Panzergrenadier-Division 'Horst Wessel', and the 8 SS-Kavallerie-Division 'Florian Geyer' had taken up positions in Hungary.

(**Above**) A Totenkopf unit pose for the camera in the snow with their commanding officer. All the men are still wearing the Type I plain tree summer camouflage tunic, which indicates the lack of winter provisions, even for one of the premier Waffen-SS divisions like Totenkopf.

(**Left**) During winter operations in early 1942 and a winter-clad signalman is operating a portable radio (*Tornisterfunkgerät* or *TornFu*). This was the standard radio system used at battalion and regimental level.

(**Opposite**) Two photographs taken during operations in the Demyansk pocket in February 1942. At Demyansk the Totenkopf were employed in the most hard-pressed areas. Two of its Kampfgruppen were used as fire brigade units, plugging gaps wherever they appeared in the front.

Totenkopf troops on the move in late February 1942 in the region of Demyansk. The battle reached its climax at the end of the month when strong Soviet forces attacked Eicke's western sector in the pocket.

A Totenkopf ski trooper halts his dogsled in the snow. By mid-January 1942 the situation in Army Group North had become critical. Field Marshal Ritter von Leeb believed that the only course of action was to withdraw over the River Lovat and form a strong defensive line. When Leeb requested permission to withdraw, Hitler refused outright, and ordered the soldiers to stand fast. As a consequence, two German corps were squeezed into the Demyansk Pocket as Red Army formations counterattacked and broke through along the River Lovat.

One of the many casualties sustained during the Demyansk action in March 1942. Here a horse-drawn sled transports an injured soldier to the rear.

A column of horse-drawn infantry trudge through the snow during bitter fighting in the Demyansk Pocket.

Soldiers taking shelter. In 1942 German troops were still learning how to deal with some of the problems of winter warfare. Both men are wearing their 'winter whites', and one is wearing his white camouflaged M1935 steel helmet. One is wearing a headpiece made from white cloth material. This was designed to help contain as much body heat as possible and to prevent discomfort from the arctic temperatures while wearing the steel helmet. Troops often complained that the helmets were like 'freezer boxes' during the winter. Heat loss through the head could lead to hypothermia.

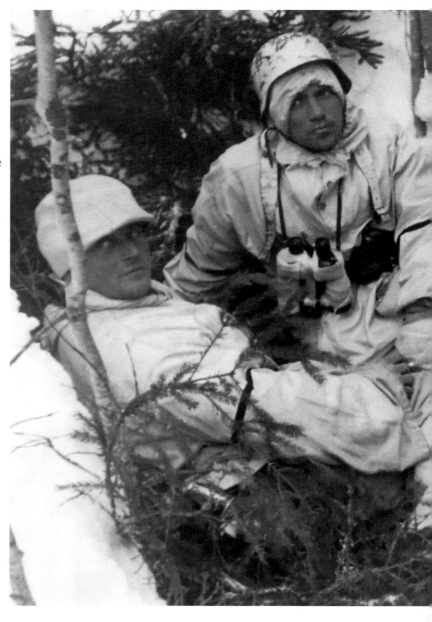

(**Opposite, above**) Inside undergrowth and a light MG34 machine gunner can be seen. Behind the machine gunner is a section leader armed with the MP38/40 sub-machine gun. They are all wearing the two-piece snow camouflage suit, and the section leader wears a coloured armband on his left arm. This enabled German troops to distinguish between friend and foe. Generally the armband was green but it could be changed in colour or position depending on the frequently changing security sequence.

(**Opposite, below**) A mortar crew preparing for a fire mission during defensive action in the Demyansk Pocket. Note the number of discarded ammunition boxes, indicating the degree of fighting raging in the area.

(**Above**) An MG34 crew on a sustained-fire Lafette 34 mount in a defensive position on the edge of the Demyansk Pocket. The gunner uses a grip trigger that has a mechanical linkage to the trigger on the gun.

(**Opposite, above**) Igloos were often built for shelter in the snow. In this photograph a light MG34 gunner can be seen preparing for a fire mission from inside the igloo.

(**Opposite, below**) Local peasants from the Demyansk region are seen huddled together, probably been displaced from their homes due to the severity of the fighting in the area.

A Totenkopf soldier during operations inside the Demyansk Pocket in February 1942. This SS man has been kitted out with ample winter clothing. The Totenkopf had received a large shipment of winter gear just before the pocket was closed, which was delivered from the massive SS supply dump established at Riga in the Baltic State of Latvia.

(**Opposite, above**) Totenkopf troops belonging to Eicke's Kampfgruppe patrol the edge of the Demyansk Pocket on horseback. A village in the background can be seen coming under attack.

(**Opposite, below**) A heavy MG34 on a sustained-fire mount somewhere in the Demyansk Pocket in February 1942. As the Soviets closed the ring around Demyansk, Totenkopf troops trapped inside were split into two Kampfgruppen. Eicke, who was ordered to defend the southwest sector of the pocket, commanded the first Kampfgruppe. On the northwest edge of the pocket, SS Oberführer Max Simon commanded the second Kampfgruppe.

During a lull in the fighting, a Totenkopf mortar crew take time out to have a much-needed cigarette. They are all wearing the two-piece snowsuit and their steel helmets have received an application of whitewash for camouflage.

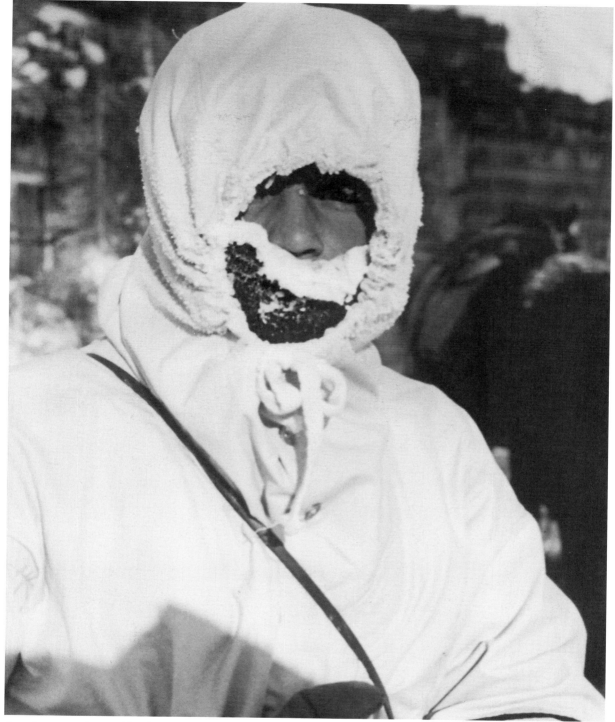

A well wrapped up soldier in a white camouflage smock. The SS, along with their regular army counterparts, made great sacrifices during the winter of 1941–42. Those that managed to survive the ordeal got a medal to prove they had been there. Troops nicknamed it the 'Frozen Meat Medal'.

(**Opposite, above**) Life in the line for Totenkopf in the Demyansk Pocket was a continuous grind of guard duties and patrolling. There was little respite.

(**Opposite, below**) A mortar crew in action in the Demyansk Pocket. The mortar was used extensively by the premier Waffen-SS divisions, as it was with all German formations. It was light, easy to carry, and gave the infantryman his own portable light artillery support.

(**Above**) Infantry take cover from the extreme temperatures wearing their winter whites. All the men are wearing the two-piece snowsuit. The white jacket had white buttons and the garment could easily be removed.

On a sled and a winter-dressed signalman is operating a portable Tornisterfunkgerät or TornFu.

A signalman probably in a forward observation post with his portable field telephone. The signals personnel were usually equipped with a variety of radio sets, field telephone sets, ten-line subscriber networks and teleprinters, as well as transmitters and receivers of several strengths.

On an icy road infantrymen pass the snow-covered bodies of soldiers killed in action. The men wear a one-piece loosing fitting snow sheet with collar and sleeve. This item of clothing had been purposely made long and the shirttails designed to reach down to the wearer's ankles. They were popular during the first winter on the Eastern Front. The soldier not only blended well with the local terrain, but was able to move more freely than with the snow sheet. The wearer's personal equipment too was worn outside the garment and this allowed the soldier easy access to his specialized equipment.

SS men are well protected against the harsh elements and are seen wearing their winter whites with scarves wrapped around their faces to combat the freezing temperatures. The soldier in the foreground can be seen wearing his carbines for his 98K bolt action rifle which is slung over his back.

(**Opposite, above**) Sprawled across the snow are dead soldiers killed during the action in the Demyansk Pocket. In almost every area on the edge of the pocket, the Totenkopf were outnumbered by the Soviets, but they had become masters in defence and beat off many enemy attacks inflicting heavy casualties.

(**Opposite, below**) A well-kitted patrol prepares to move out for an overnight mission, which is why they are carrying blankets. In the brutal winter months the troops would often endure weeks without removing their winter suits. There were no opportunities to wash and white camouflage soon became so filthy that it no longer had effective concealment.

A patrol can be seen on the move. The section leader, who can be seen with the black and red button-on arm strips to identify friend or foe, is armed with the MP38/40 sub-machine gun.

Wearing their dirty snow shirts this light MG34 squad prepare to move out during operations in February 1942.

A patrol preparing to move out on a night mission.

A cold solider still retaining his summer kit, but padded out with layers of clothing, is seen trying to keep warm next to an improvised shelter in some undergrowth. Beneath his M1938 field cap he wears a black woollen toque to keep his head warm.

(**Above**) A Totenkopf donned in his winter whites, while the other soldier wears the new winter reversible, grey side out. This garment, the first truly reversible winter weather uniform, introduced on the Eastern Front in 1942, was designed large enough to be worn over the soldier's field service uniform, including the basic field equipment. However, most soldiers preferred wearing their equipment over the winter jacket.

(**Opposite, above**) Two troop leaders armed with the 9mm MP40 machine pistol, normally issued only to squad or platoon leaders. They are both clad in their winter whites over their standard army issue greatcoats. Attached to their black leather belts are map cases, and the man on the right can be seen with ammunition pouches which held 32-round magazines. The soldier on the left is armed with a Stg 24 stick hand grenade carried in his belt.

(**Opposite, below**) Preparing for a night patrol with all their supplies on sleds. Most of these riflemen wear the two-piece snow suit. By 1942 manufacturers were designing new, more practical winter camouflage garments. One such item was the first two-piece snowsuit, comprising a snow-jacket and matching trousers. The jacket, buttoned all the way down the front with white painted buttons, had a large white hood which could easily be pulled over the steel helmet.

Totenkopf troops in the snow with a stationary Pz.Kpfw.III during operations in the Demyansk Pocket in March 1942.

In the Demyansk Pocket and Totenkopf troops wearing their winter whites are seen with a Wehrmacht radio operator. Note a roll of cable and the portable 'TornFu'. These radios were carried on a specially designed backpack frame, and when connected to each other (upper and lower valves) via special cables, could be used on the march. The rapid transmission of orders and the fast action taken in response to them were key to the successes enjoyed by the Germans during the war.

During an enemy contact, these riflemen, wearing the early version of winter whites, are keeping low to the snow while a mortar crew are seen preparing their weapon for action. Some of the troops are armed with the Kar 98k, known variously as a Gewehr (rifle, even though it was technically a carbine), the Mauserbuchse (Buchse was an old term for a firearm), Mauserkarabiner (Mauser carbine), Flinte (shotgun), or Knarre (a colloquialism for gun).

An infantry patrol and a light MG34 squad wearing their winter whites can be seen with their sleds in the snow.

(**Above**) More than likely the same patrol as the last photograph, this time showing infantry wearing their winter whites with their Kar 98K bolt action rifles thrown over their backs. The troops are wearing early snow garments. While this provided good freedom of movement, especially while skiing, it did not offer adequate protection against the extreme cold. The men are all wearing the standard equipment for a rifleman with the usual belt and cartridge pouches hidden under their garment.

(**Opposite, above**) In a captured Russian trench and two riflemen can be seen preparing for action. The soldier rests his standard 7.9mm Kar 98K on what appears to be a discarded ammunition box.

(**Opposite, below**) Totenkopf troops examine a knocked-out whitewashed Soviet tank during operations in the Demyansk Pocket in March 1942. Note how dirty their winter whites have become.

An infantry advance is in progress and two soldiers, wearing the winter reversible white side out, are moving forward through some woods being supported by a Pz.Kpfw.III.

A motley assortment of troops along a trench during the winter of 1942. Some members of the Totenkopf can be seen wearing the reversible winter smocks grey side out.

Chapter Three

Bitter Fighting
(1941–44)

By October 1941, Totenkopf had been weakened by its defensive action. The division had suffered some 6,600 casualties with only 2,500 replacements since the invasion had started. The division was still ordered to advance East, even though it could only really perform defensive fighting. East of Lushno the units were once again embroiled in heavy fighting and halted against repeated strong Soviet resistance. To add to the problems on the battlefield cold driving rain fell on the front and within hours the Russian countryside had been turned into a quagmire with roads and fields becoming virtually impassable. Although tanks and other tracked vehicles managed to push through the mire at slow pace, animal draft, trucks and other wheeled vehicles became hopelessly stuck. To make matters worse, German supply lines were becoming increasingly overstretched, their vehicles were breaking down, and casualty returns were mounting. When the snow arrived, the front had stagnated and Totenkopf troops dug in for the winter. The Russians, as predicted, finally ran out of power because of the harsh weather, and were unable to achieve any penetration into the German lines – this saved the front from destruction.

Following the traumatic winter of 1941, the German leadership were determined that 1942 would bring a successful outcome to the campaign in the Soviet Union. Yet, the New Year opened with the German army struggling for survival. The 'Das Reich' Division for instance, which had fought in front of Moscow, had lost more than half of its fighting strength. Further north on the Leningrad Front, the Totenkopf Division had fared not much better and were embroiled in heavy fighting, again in the region of Demyansk.

By early February 1942, some 95,000 German troops had become trapped in the 'Demyansk Pocket'. Throughout March, fighting continued to rage with German troops trying in vain to escape the pocket. It was not until April that a bridgehead was finally established between the soldiers in the pocket and the rest of Army Group North. The survival of the Totenkopf trapped inside the pocket was a great achievement and contributed significantly to the stabilization of the German position around Lake Ilmen.

Through the rest of the year they were to continue to wage a battle of attrition against their irrepressible foe, and even began to respect their determination and tenacity. Yet in spite winning a number of successful battles against the Red Army it soon became apparent to the German leadership that there would be no victory that year.

By early 1943, the SS divisions on the Eastern Front had been numbered and some had been upgraded to full Panzer status. The Waffen-SS represented around five percent of the fighting strength of the German forces and more than a quarter of all its Panzer forces. The 'classic' SS divisions – Leibstandarte, Das Reich, Totenkopf, Polizei, Wiking and Nord – had all played their part in the war on the Eastern Front and were now overstretched. To alleviate its manpower shortages the Waffen-SS recruited foreign soldiers into newly created Waffen-SS divisions.

In February 1943 the Soviets were intoxicated by their victory at Stalingrad and Hitler was resolute not to allow Kharkov to fall into enemy hands. The task of carrying out the battle for Kharkov was given to SS-Obergruppenführer Paul 'Papa' Hausser's newly created II SS-Panzer-Korps. Hausser's SS-Korps was ordered to fight to the death inside the rubble strewn city, but after days of continuous combat were compelled to evacuate it, much to the anger of Hitler.

On 4 March, determined to retake Kharkov, the 4th Panzer Army joined forces with the II SS-Panzer-Korps and 'Das Reich' and launched a massive attack penetrating the outskirts of the city. To the north the Leibstandarte's Panzer Regiments I and II smashed their way into Kharkov. Fierce fighting ensued and as Soviet forces escaped onto the Kharkov–Belgorod road, Totenkopf troops were there ready to annihilate them.

The victory at Kharkov was now complete. The victory had come with a heavy price in blood, with some 12,000 soldiers killed, but with the city retaken, Hitler now confidently planned a new offensive against the Kursk salient. Here Hitler was confronted with a tempting strategic opportunity that would, he predicted, deliver him victory.

On 5 July 1943, the II SS-Panzer-Korps, which comprised the 'Leibstandarte', 'Das Reich' and 'Totenkopf' Divisions, attacked in the pre-dawn light along the Kursk salient. The task of the SS-Panzer-Korps was to advance via Beresov and Sadeynoye and smash through the first defensive belt. After this was achieved the next objective was to break through the second line of Russian positions between Lutchki and Jakovlevo. Once these were destroyed the advance would follow in a north-easterly direction. For this operation the 167 Infanterie-Division would form part of the SS Korps and would guard the left flank.

The soldiers of the Totenkopf division wasted no time and smashed a series of strong Soviet defence lines. Das Reich also made progress and by evening of the first day Totenkopf, Leibstandarte and Das Reich had in some places penetrated 13 miles into the Russian defences. Over the next few days the advance continued to go well with Totenkopf smashing its way through more than 30 miles of Russian line, while Leibstandarte and Das Reich were equally successful, despite heavy casualties.

On 9 July, the SS-Panzer-Korps continued heavy fighting against strong enemy forces. Although in danger of being cut off and encircled, they pushed forward and attacked Soviet troops northeast of Beregovoy. During the advance, Das Reich guarded the eastern flank of Totenkopf and Leibstandarte. En route on 12 July it became embroiled in bitter fighting in a huge tank battle in the hills around Prokhorovka. Here the Soviet 5th Guard and 5th Guard Tank Armies clashed with the powerful armoured SS units which was the climax of Operation Zitadelle.

During the showdown the SS remained on the defensive, repelling a number of armoured and infantry attacks. Less than a week after the start of Zitadelle, both sides had lost several hundred tanks and thousands of troops. Although Russian losses in both men and equipment far exceeded the German, their losses could be replaced. German losses, except where armour could be recovered, were not replaceable. The SS divisions, Leibstandarte, Das Reich and Totenkopf, had lost more than half their vehicles and taken massive casualties. The Red Army had suffered much higher losses with some 177,000 being killed and injured, and a staggering 2,586 tanks and self-propelled guns lost during the battle.

By 13 July, the II SS-Panzer-Korps was unable to make any further progress, and poor ground conditions were hampering its logistics. Despite efforts to batter their way through, SS troops had neither the strength nor resources to do so. The cream of the German Panzer force, so carefully concentrated before the operation, was exhausted and the Russians had gained the initiative in the east. The campaign in Russia would now consist of a series of German withdrawals, with the Waffen-SS contesting every inch of the way.

In the southern sector of the Eastern Front, German troops frantically withdrew as Russian forces smashed through the Mius defences and advanced at speed towards Stalino and Taganrog, along the northern coast of the Sea of Azov. Although SS troops of Das Reich and Totenkopf distinguished themselves with their bravery, they could only manage to stem the Red Army for short periods of time.

By mid-August 1943, the Russians had wrenched open a huge gap in the German lines west of Kursk, once again threatening to retake the important industrial city of Kharkov. Das Reich, Totenkopf and Wiking divisions were thrown into battle to prevent the loss of the city. Although all these combat formations were weakened by the Zitadelle disaster, they were still a formidable fighting force. The city had only been recaptured by the Waffen-SS in March 1943, and now it was the Red Army's turn to launch a pincer attack to capture it back again.

Within days of the SS redeployment to Kharkov the Russian 53rd Army driving from north and the 57th Army advancing from the south attacked the city in strength.

Over the next few days the SS scored some outstanding successes in localized combats with Russian armoured units, but, with acute shortages in men and equipment the situation deteriorated by the day.

By early September Hitler grudgingly decided to allow troops to pull out of the doomed city. By early September, with ever increasing losses in men and material, Kharkov was finally evacuated and the SS undertook a spirited withdrawal towards the River Dnieper. Here they managed to halt the Russian onslaught towards the river, allowing Manstein's forces to retreat and redeploy.

Throughout the weeks that followed, German front lines were pulled farther westwards with SS units defending, attacking and counter-attacking as the situation demanded. Their new role as the so-called 'fire brigades', being shuttled from one danger spot to another to face down Russian attacks, typified their position during late 1943.

By early January 1944 the situation on the Eastern Front for the SS had deteriorated in spite its distinguished performance. The Totenkopf were tasked with defending the Dnieper near Krivoi Rog. Fighting along the river was remorseless and losses were high. During their defence the division found itself embroiled in the relief of German troops in what became known as the Korsun Pocket.

Along the German front, Totenkopf troops were experiencing problems in many areas and in spite of strongly held positions, which were manned with an assortment of Pak guns and lines of machine gun pits, the Red Army moved forward in their hundreds regardless of the cost in life, squeezing the pocket. All along the battered front, SS troops tried in vain to hold their positions against overwhelming odds.

In the second week of March, following a ferocious battle near Kirovograd, Totenkopf troops reluctantly fell back behind the Bug. Here they continued their defence. Already the Russian advance in the south had brought its armies perilously close to the borders of Hungary. Before panic had spread across the southern front, Hitler had ordered Operation Margarethe – the German occupation of Hungary. The operation largely involved Waffen-SS and second-rate SS combat formations being used as 'fire brigade' units. By April 1944, the 16 SS-Panzergrenadier-Division 'Reichsführer-SS', the 18 SS-Panzergrenadier-Division 'Horst Wessel', and the 8 SS-Kavallerie-Division 'Florian Geyer' had taken up positions in Hungary.

(**Opposite, above**) During winter operations in early 1943 and Totenkopf troops are digging in during a defensive action. Note the FlaK gun mounted on the halftrack. With the vehicle's folding sides down the gun was adaptable and could traverse 360 degrees.

(**Opposite, below**) A 5cm Panzerabwehrkanone (Pak) 38 in action against an enemy target. These anti-tank guns were found in all the premier Waffen-SS divisions during this period and were capable of disabling heavy Soviet tanks.

A 2cm FlaK gun during winter operations on the Eastern Front. The gunner has used white sheeting to drape over the splinter shield to break up its distinctive shape and to camouflage it.

Inside a shelter during the Kharkov offensive in March 1943 and an MG34 heavy machine gunner can be seen during a firing mission.

Moving forward towards Kharkov a Totenkopf light MG34 machine gun crew. The machine gun has the MG34 50-round basket drum magazine fitted. Rifle groups generally carried a bipod and one or two spare barrels.

During the opening phase of the battle of Kharkov, an MG34 is mounted on the Lafette 34 tripod which weighed 20.5kg. The optimum crew of an MG34 for sustained-fire operation was six men. The gunner was the No. 1, the No. 2 carried the tripod, and Nos 3, 4, and 5 carried ammunition, spare barrels, entrenching tools, and other items. The Nos 1 and 2 were armed with pistols, while the remaining three carried rifles. The team was often reduced to just to two or three (as in this photograph): the gunner, the loader/barrel carrier, and the spotter. The gunner was normally a junior NCO.

Totenkopf troops moving through Kharkov in March 1943. The soldiers all wear the reversible winter jacket and trouser. The clothing consisted of a heavy reversible double-breasted overjacket designed for extra frontal warmth. It had double-buttoned overlaps at the front, which when closed were wind resistant. The bottom edge of the jacket had drawstrings and the ends of the cuffs were also adjustable. The trousers were thick, as was the jacket, and reversible. They were shorter than standard issue uniform trousers but could be either worn over the top of the leather marching boots or tucked inside. The ends of the trousers were gathered in by drawstrings and tied in around the boots. The winter reversible was normally mouse-grey on one side and winter white on the other.

A PaK gun crew in March 1943. Note the Unterscharführer or assault gun leader armed with the 9mm MP40 machine pistol who is wearing a typical reversible parka grey side out with his trousers white side out. By the winter of 1942/43 the Germans had developed a new revolutionary item of clothing for Waffen-SS troops and armoured crews, called the parka. It was well-made and well-padded and kept crews warm. It was first designed in field-grey with a reversible winter white, but by late 1943 a new modification was made by replacing the field-grey side with a camouflage pattern, either in green splinter or tan water. The coat was double-breasted.

(**Above**) A Totenkopf patrol preparing to move out during the battle of Kharkov. A stationary SS whitewashed Pz.Kpfw.III tank crew can be seen preparing for an armoured assault. On 4 March, determined to retake Kharkov, the 4th Panzer Army joined forces with the I SS Panzer Corps and launched a massive attack. Das Reich penetrated the outskirts of Kharkov to the north and the Leibstandarte and Panzer-Regiments I and II smashed their way into the city. Fierce fighting ensued, and as Soviet forces escaped onto the Kharkov–Belgorad road Totenkopf troops were there ready to annihilate them.

(**Opposite, above**) A motorcyclist has halted at a temporary fuel depot outside the city of Kharkov. Note the 20-litre fuel cans that were distributed among the units from the main fuel drums.

(**Opposite, below**) Grenadiers hitch a lift on an armoured vehicle belonging to the II SS Panzer Corps as it negotiates its advance through the streets of Kharkov. The battle of Kharkov was a series of battles launched by the Germans that began on 19 February 1943, to take advantage of the fact that the Red Army had exhausted much of its strength and overrun its supply lines following the massive series of offensives it had launched against the Germans during its victory at Stalingrad in early February.

(**Above**) Totenkopf troops unloading a 10.5cm howitzer off a flatbed railcar during battle of Kharkov. The 10.5cm light field howitzer was used extensively on the Eastern Front and provided the division with a versatile, comparatively mobile base of fire.

(**Opposite, above**) On the Eastern Front in March 1943 and the crew of a Pz.Kpfw.III can be seen wearing their parka reversible jackets grey side out.

(**Opposite, below**) Following the harsh winter of early 1943 came the thaw. In this photograph a Totenkopf motorcycle combination struggles along a muddy road.

On patrol and troops can be seen wearing the Type II camouflage smock. This smock was a much-improved design: it was slimmer, the wrist band was raised, and there were two extra pockets below the waist band. This pattern shown in mid-war blurred edge. As with the Type I, all smocks were made reversible from the spring to the autumn.

Totenkopf troops are seen on the advance through Russia in June 1943. Following the victory at Kharkov, Totenkopf was shifted to Kursk to take part in Operation Zitadelle.

A stationary Panzerkampfwagen VI Tiger Ausf H of the 9th Schwere SS Panzer Kompanie Totenkopf, tank number 932, during the Kursk offensive in 1943.

A junior assault leader, or SS-Untersturmführer, is seen with his unit in a trench during the battle of Kursk in July 1943. This initial phase of the fighting had been costly to the Russians, but in a tactical and operational sense it achieved its objectives. During the days that followed the Red Army began to deprive the SS of tactical superiority.

Troops moving into action across a field. At their starting positions, the three SS premier divisions covered a sector that was 12 miles wide. The Totenkopf occupied the left flank of the advance, the Leibstandarte was in the centre and Das Reich held the right. It was hoped that these premier Waffen-SS divisions would play a decisive part in the victory at Kursk.

A group of Totenkopf troops pose for the camera next to a support vehicle during the Kursk offensive. By the end of the first day of the battle, the Germans had broken through the first line of Soviet defences and created a gap almost 10 miles wide and 5 miles deep. Fighting intensified as the Germans exploited the receding front lines.

Two photographs showing armoured vehicles and SS troops spread out across the landscape during the battle of the Kursk. This battle was probably the first modern Soviet operation of the war. Even though the Red Army lacked technological superiority, they had a well-prepared defensive programme, which included elaborate deception plans to confuse the enemy.

A Pz.Kpfw.IV Ausf G with tactical number 921 of 3rd SS Panzergrenadier Division Totenkopf at Kursk in July 1943. The Pz.Kpfw.IV played a prominent role during the Kursk offensive. Despite inferior numbers, the tank performed well in various operations, and achieved resounding success especially for the elite Waffen-SS divisions.

(**Opposite, above**) A light MG42 gun crew have disembarked from their Schwimmwagen and go into action. Troops appreciated the value of the MG42 and when times and conditions allowed, crews prepared several firing positions.

(**Opposite, below**) 7.5cm l.IG18 gunners in action. This weapon was used in direct infantry support. It was versatile in combat and the crew often aggressively positioned it, meaning that it was exposed on the battlefield.

A Tiger tank being rearmed. The Tiger entered service in August 1942 and soon gained a superb fighting record. The mighty Tigers played a key role in the German offensive at Kursk.

(**Opposite, above**) Totenkopf troops passing burning Russian vehicles during the Kursk offensive.

(**Opposite, below**) Onboard an Sd.Kfz.251 an MG42 machine gunner can be seen training his weapon on an enemy target. Despite the Panzerwaffe's impressive array of firepower at Kursk, there was a shortage of infantry which led to Panzer units being required to take on tasks normally reserved for the infantry.

Troops pose for the camera next to an HF12 mobile kitchen wagon.

A FlaK crew pose for the camera with their 2cm gun. By the time the Kursk offensive began both the Heer and Waffen-SS mechanized formations had a plentiful supply of these guns.

Totenkopf troops pose for the camera in the summer of 1943 following the battle of Kursk. During the battle Totenkopf had lost more than half its tanks and vehicles and taken huge casualties.

A PaK 35/36 crew during a defensive action. Following the failure of Kursk German forces were now on the defensive. In the southern sector of the Eastern Front troops frantically withdrew as Russian forces smashed through the Mius defences and advanced towards Stalino and Taganrog along the northern coast of the Sea of Azov. Although troops of Das Reich and Totenkopf distinguished themselves with their bravery, they could only manage to stem the Red Army for short periods.

(**Opposite, above**) Totenkopf troops poised for action during fighting in the summer of 1943. During August Totenkopf was moved north, back to Kharkov. Along with Das Reich, it took part in the battles to halt Operation Rumyantsev in a desperate attempt to halt the Soviet capture of the city. The city was abandoned on 23 August due to the threats on the German flanks.

(**Opposite, below**) Totenkopf soldiers move across some boggy terrain armed with their 9mm machine pistols. Totenkopf and Das Reich had been given orders to try to prevent the Russian drive on the Dnieper, and then stop the Soviet tanks from wheeling south and threatening Kharkov. In mid-August these Waffen-SS divisions tried in vain to stop the Russian drive, but by 22 August, overwhelmed by Soviet superiority, Kharkov was captured.

(**Above**) On the front line is a 2cm FlaK 38 quadruple mount. This gun could fire a lethal 1,800 rounds per minute from its four barrels. One man fired the top left and bottom right guns while another fired the top right and bottom left. The loader changed the magazines while the others continued to fire.

An SS troop leader wearing his Type II summer camouflage smock. His M1935 helmet has been heavily camouflaged. He is wearing around his neck a pair of 6 × 30 Zeiss binoculars.

(**Opposite, above**) Troops on the defensive with their bolt-action rifles. In spite the loss of Kharkov, Totenkopf's success in halting the Russian advance on the Dnieper had helped to prevent a major disaster on the Eastern Front. However by the end of August the division had withdrawn to the western bank.

(**Opposite, below**) Totenkopf troops boarding an inflatable boat crossing the Dnieper at the end of August 1943.

(**Opposite, above**) Totenkopf troops near a rail line in October 1943. During the first week of October, the Russians launched an attack against the Germans in the bend of the Dnieper between Kremenchug and Zaporozhye. Its forces hit the Germans so hard that they broke across the river onto the west bank forcing both Heer and Waffen-SS forces to withdraw.

(**Opposite, below**) Troops pause in the fighting to have a well-earned beer before resuming operations.

(**Above**) An MG34 Panzergrenadier squad during operations in late November 1943. By this time, Totenkopf had been reduced to three full battalions of Panzergrenadiers, one weak battalion of tanks, just over half its artillery and FlaK, and half its engineer battalion, but it was nearly full strength in supply and support units.

(**Opposite, above**) A Totenkopf during a fire mission in December 1943. The versatile 8.8cm FlaK continued to be used in a dual role of anti-aircraft and anti-personnel until the end of the war. It was used extensively during the defensive actions along the banks of the Dneiper.

(**Opposite, below**) A commander inside his cupola watches a burning Russian tank near Krivoi Rog. Here Totenkopf fought doggedly to hold the city from falling into Russian hands. It would not be until February 1944 that it fell.

(**Above**) Near the city of Krivoi Rog and Totenkopf troops rest in the snow during operations in January 1944.

Chapter Four

End Game
(1944–45)

By mid-1944 the situation for Totenkopf soldiers on the Eastern Front was bleak. They had fought desperately to maintain cohesion, plugged gaps in the front, relieved German soldiers surrounded or cut off, and recaptured towns and villages that were heavily fortified. By the summer of 1944 German forces were holding a battle line 1,400 miles long.

Units were no longer being refitted with replacements to compensate for the large losses sustained. Supplies of equipment and ammunition were insufficient and commanders were compelled to ration supplies. Many soldiers, even the most battle-hardened, were becoming aware that they were in the final stages of the war in the east. They had realized that they were now fighting an enemy that were far superior to them. The Red Army were constantly outgunning them, and now Luftwaffe air support was almost non-existent. The short summer nights too had caused problems, for they only had a few hours of darkness in which to conceal their night marches and construct fortifications. Ultimately, the Totenkopf, and indeed any of the Waffen-SS premier divisions in the summer of 1944, was ill-prepared to face a large-scale offensive.

The long awaited Soviet summer offensive, codenamed Operation Bagration, was finally unleashed on 22 June against Army Group Centre. Vast sections of the front erupted in a wall of flame and smoke. Almost 22,000 guns and mortars and 2,000 Katyusha multiple rocket launchers poured fire and destruction onto the German defensive positions. Some German soldiers, in their confusion, scrambled out of their trenches to save themselves from the rain of bombs. The Germans found that the Red Army were using new tactics. In other battles the Russians had attacked on a broad front with minimal artillery support. Now they had adopted the German use of attack by concentrating large numbers of infantry supported by heavy artillery and armour. From various observation posts dug along the front the Germans found that the Red Army attacked more heavily defended positions first before bringing up the assault groups. Once the assault groups made contact the armoured forces were then sent in to break through the lines.

Totenkopf had been ordered to join the 4th Army to try to hold positions to the west of Army Group Centre. By 4 July the absence of communications made it impossible for the Germans to accurately assess the situation, but it was becoming clear that it was calamitous and the front was caving in. There seemed no stopping the tide of the Russian advance. Engagements like this had been fought scores of times on the Eastern Front, but never with such ferocity. While some areas still held fanatically, a general breakdown began to sweep the lines. German soldiers were stunned by the force of the blow that had hit Army Group Centre. After more than ten days fighting, areas that still remained in German hands were reduced to a few shrinking pockets of resistance.

Totenkopf units were shifted to defensive positions in the city of Grodno to hold the right flank of 4th Army in the north and left wing of the 2nd Army in the south. For eleven days, outnumbered, its units held on until finally it had to withdraw and retreat towards Warsaw. Battered and bruised the division slowly retreated around the Polish capital.

On 11 September Totenkopf managed to fight off Soviet forces in the north-eastern suburbs of Warsaw. It fought fanatically and skillfully and held the Russians back for almost ten days. This victory provided a temporary lull which allowed Totenkopf to dig in. The Red Army's troops were exhausted and their armoured vehicles were in need of maintenance and repair. Totenkopf and its Army counterparts were spared from being driven out of Poland for the time being.

While the front east of the Polish capital was temporarily stabilized, elsewhere on the Eastern Front the situation was dire. The 2nd Ukrainian Front had broken through powerful German defences supported by heavy armour, and had reached the Bulgarian border on 1 September. Within a week, Soviet troops reached the Yugo-slav frontier. On 8 September, Bulgaria and Romania then declared war on Germany. Two weeks later, on 23 September, Soviet forces arrived on the Hungarian border and raced through the country for the Danube, reaching the river to the south of Budapest.

General Otto Wöhler's Army Group South was committed to the defence of the Hungarian capital, including the 22 SS Freiwilligen-Kavallerie-Division 'Maria Theresia' and 18 SS-Freiwilligen-Panzergrenadier-Division 'Horst Wessel'. These SS forces were not only employed to protect Budapest, but were also there to retain law and order and suppress any local uprisings. However in October 1944, as news reached the capital that the Red Army had crossed the Hungarian frontier and were advancing towards the Danube in the direction of Budapest, Hitler knew that it would fall without additional support and wasted no time ordering his premier SS divisions to Hungary. The Waffen-SS forces positioned along the Vistula in Poland were to be transferred to Hungary.

On 26 December, the 6th Panzer-Corps, comprising Totenkopf and Wiking, were transferred from the Warsaw area and given orders to relieve Budapest. The attack was scheduled to begin on New Year's Day. Two attempts were made to relieve the city but the 6th Panzer-Corps was beaten back by Soviet forces. For the next five weeks Totenkopf and Wiking were forced onto the defensive and could only watch the beleaguered garrison struggle against Red Army attacks.

On 11 February 1945, the remaining SS troops trapped inside the city attempted to breakout to the west. In the terrible battles that ensued, the fleeing SS troops of 'Florian Geyer' and 'Maria Theresia' were virtually annihilated. Out of the 30,000 SS troops that tried to escape, only some 700 reached the 6th Panzer-Corps lines. By 12 February Budapest was comfortably in Russian hands.

The remnants of both of the decimated SS foreign volunteer divisions were absorbed to form the 37th SS-Freiwilligen-Kavallerie-Division 'Lützow'. The SS division, which never reached the strength of a single regiment, was soon to be on the front lines fighting alongside the 6th SS-Panzer-Army in a new plan aimed at retaking Budapest. The plan, codenamed 'Spring Awakening', involved attacks by Wöhler's Army Group South, which would consist of the 6th SS-Panzer-Army, 8th Army, 6th Army and the Hungarian 3rd Army. The German and Hungarian force would attack south from Margarethe defence lines, while Army Group South 2nd Army would attack from the west of the Russian lines. The planned pincer movement would crush the 3rd Ukrainian Front. The 6th SS-Panzer-Army would remain in the Margarethe positions around Lake Balaton. The Panzer-Korps was commanded by SS-Oberstgruppenführer 'Sepp' Dietrich and consisted of the Leibstandarte, Das Reich, Hohenstaufen and Hitlerjugend divisions. These SS divisions were all newly arrived from the Ardennes offensive.

During the early hours of the morning on 6 March 1945, Operation Spring Awakening was initiated. Leibstandarte, Das Reich, Totenkopf, Wiking, Hohenstaufen and Hitlerjugend divisions crashed into action with all the customary determination and élan expected of them. However, almost immediately Totenkopf came up against stiff resistance, and by 13 March the offensive came to a halt. The German soldiers were soaked, freezing and exhausted, and the Russians pounded them mercilessly. To avoid total destruction a general retreat by the Waffen-SS, much to the anger of Hitler, was ordered towards the Austrian border.

Following the loss of Hungary, the bulk of the Waffen-SS withdrew into Austria to defend Vienna. Totenkopf helped in the defensive battle around the Austrian capital, but it was soon realized that if the division remained holding the city, it would be annihilated. Reluctantly, the division, along with remnants of other premier Waffen-SS troops and Heer forces, withdrew west. On 13 April, the Red Army marched into Vienna.

In the closing days of the war most German soldiers desired to withdraw west and surrender to the Anglo-American forces rather than the Red Army. The Totenkopf finally capitulated to the Americans on 9 May.

The SS had battled across half of Russia, they had shown their skill and endurance at Kursk and Kharkov, and gone on to protect the withdrawals of the rest of the German Army to the gates of Warsaw, Budapest, Vienna and beyond.

However, their reputation of indiscriminately murdering PoWs and innocent civilians had left many Russians wanting to exact reprisals against the division. When Totenkopf surrendered, the Americans handed them over to the Soviets, who were determined to settle a score. Very few Totenkopf soldiers survived Russian captivity.

SS Panzergrenadiers hitch a lift aboard a Pz.Kpfw.III during operations in early 1944. The tank has evidently seen some enemy contact as it is missing some of its side-skirt.

An 8cm sGrW 34 mortar crew during a fire mission. Each SS battalion fielded some six of these excellent mortars, which could fire fifteen projectiles per minute to a range of 2,400 metres. It fired high-explosive, smoke, and 'bounding' bombs. During the war the mortar had become the standard infantry support weapon giving the soldier valuable high explosive capability beyond the range of riles or grenades. One of the drawbacks was its accuracy. Even with an experienced mortar crew, it generally required ten bombs to achieve a direct hit on a target.

(**Opposite, above**) An Sd.Kfz.251 Ausf C halftrack infantry personnel vehicle on the move in the winter of 1944. These front-wheel-steering vehicles had transformed the fighting ability of both the Heer and Waffen-SS during the war. Various halftracks were built during the war; 16,000 of the Sd.Kfz.251 variant poured off the production line between 1940 and late 1944.

(**Opposite, below**) A group of Totenkopf troops pose for the camera inside a trench in March 1943. In January Totenkopf had been engaged in defensive fighting east of the Dnieper near Krivoi Rog. In February the division took part in the relief attempt of German forces encircled in the Korsun Pocket. In the second week of March, after unrelenting fighting near Kirovograd, Totenkopf were finally forced back behind the River Bug.

(**Above**) Panzergrenadiers standing next to a Sturmgeschütz (Stug) III Ausf G during operations in early 1944. An MG42 can be seen leaning against the vehicle. An assault gun has been loaded onto a train for transportation to the Eastern Front. This vehicle is equipped with the longer-barrelled 7.5cm StuK 40 L/48 cannon, which necessitated modification of the frontal superstructure and increased its weight to 21.3 tons. Despite this, it was continually hard pressed on the battlefield and constantly called upon for offensive and defensive fire support, where it was gradually compelled to operate increasingly in an anti-tank role.

(**Opposite, above**) SS Panzergrenadiers on the march being supported by a column of Sd.Kfz.251 halftracks. The halftrack was one of the quickest ways for troops to enter the forward edge of the battlefield. Throughout the war on the Eastern Front the halftrack offered troops armoured protection and mobility. The use of the halftrack was an example of rapid tactical deployment that changed the way battle was fought forever.

(**Opposite, below**) A prime mover towing the deadly 8.8cm FlaK gun towards the front. Of all the FlaK guns that were introduced into service, the best-known and most reliable were the 8.8cm Flugabwehrkanone, versions 18, 36 and 37. All three were extensively used during the war by the Luftwaffe, Heer and later the Waffen-SS. They also used a version 41, or 8.8cm FlaK 41 (Eisenerz). This one was built specifically for a dual role and possessed a genuine anti-tank capability. Its longer barrel gave it an increased muzzle velocity and better penetration. It proved robust, reliable, and it continued in production until the end of the war.

(**Above**) An SS crew can be seen in the fighting compartment of a moving Hummel. The Hummel mounted a standard 15cm heavy field howitzer in a lightly armoured fighting compartment built on the chassis of a Pz.Kpfw.III or IV. This heavy self-propelled gun carried eighteen rounds and was a potent weapon against Soviet armour. It was popular and 666 were built until the programme was terminated in 1944.

(**Opposite, above**) Two Totenkopf Panthers inside a town on the Eastern Front, destined for the front lines. By 1944 the disparity of armoured vehicles meant that tanks like the Panther had to wage continuous defensive battles to wear down the enemy in a war of attrition.

(**Opposite, below**) Panzergrenadiers board a Pz.Kpfw.III during summer operations in 1944. On 22 June the Russians initiated Operation Bagration. Its objective was to annihilate Army Group Centre. The three German armies opposing them had thirty-seven divisions, weakly supported by armour, against 166 divisions, supported by 2,700 tanks and 1,300 assault guns. At the end of the first week of Bagration the three German armies had lost between them nearly 200,000 men and 900 tanks; 9th Army and the 3rd Panzer Army were almost wiped out. The remnants of the shattered armies trudged back west to rest, refit and build new defensive lines. Any plans to regain the initiative on the Eastern Front were doomed forever. As for Totenkopf, they became ensnarled in the rail bottleneck to Army Group Centre's west as it withdrew to join the 4th Army. By July, the division had been withdrawn into Poland to take up defensive action around the city of Grodno.

(**Above**) Totenkopf grenadiers during fighting in Poland in the summer of 1944. Spread across a field are destroyed Soviet tanks. While the Totenkopf were outnumbered seven to one in troops and ten to one in tanks, the division held on around Grodno. However, by the end of July, they were compelled to relinquish their positions and withdraw towards Poland.

(**Opposite, above**) Two Totenkopf soldiers smile for the camera as they pass through a Polish town in the summer of 1944 onboard a Schwimmwagen.

(**Opposite, below**) Smiling for the camera Totenkopf troops are seen with a motorcyclist and his motorcycle during summer operations in 1944. While there seems to be jovial antics by these men, the situation for the division, and indeed the entire German army in Poland, was dire.

A soldier hurls a stick grenade from within the fighting compartment of an Sd.Kfz.251 halftrack. Note the MG42 machine gun and splinter shield mounted on the front of the compartment.

The crew of a late model Tiger I of the 3rd SS Totenkopf Division pose for the camera in front of their vehicle after managing to take a short break from the fighting around Warsaw. The German assault pushed the Soviet forces out of the city and across the Vistula River.

Following operations around Warsaw, Totenkopf and Wiking were pulled out and sent by train via Prague, Vienna and Bratislava to western Hungary, where they were given instructions to drive on to Budapest. Here in these two photographs Totenkopf grenadiers are seen on the move towards Budapest in early 1945.

(**Above**) Totenkopf troops on the road to Budapest in January 1945. It was around Budapest that Totenkopf once again threw themselves into battle with their customary determination and élan. They launched their attack on New Year's Day, but by 13 March the advance stalled in the face of strong Russian resistance and the thaw that turned the roads and surrounding countryside into a quagmire.

(**Opposite**) In a trench and these Totenkopf troops are being subjected to merciless Soviet aerial and ground bombardment. The German soldiers were soaked, freezing and exhausted. Totenkopf fought on, but found themselves overwhelmed by enemy superiority in numbers of soldiers and weapons. To prevent total destruction, a general retreat by Totenkopf and Wiking ensued, much to the anger of Hitler. Following the loss of Hungary, the bulk of the Waffen-SS withdrew into Austria to defend Vienna. Totenkopf helped in the defensive battle around the Austrian capital, but it was a token resistance, as two huge Soviet fronts converged on the city.

Appendix

Organizational History of Totenkopf

Totenkopf Division (formed 16 October 1939 in Dachau)

1st SS Totenkopf Infantry Regiment
2nd SS Totenkopf Infantry Regiment
3rd SS Totenkopf Infantry Regiment
SS Totenkopf Reconnaissance Battalion
SS Totenkopf Panzerabwehr (anti-tank) Battalion
SS Totenkopf Artillery Regiment
SS Totenkopf Pioneer Battalion
SS Totenkopf Signals Battalion

During winter 1939 the division added the 4th SS Totenkopf Artillery Regiment, which was a heavy battalion.

Added 1942 added

SS Totenkopf FlaK Battalion
SS Totenkopf Feldersatz Battalion
Thule Schützen Regiment

In November 1942, following heavy casualties on the Eastern France, it was moved to France for a refit. It was organized into the SS Totenkopf Panzer Grenadier Division and 3rd SS Panzer Division Totenkopf:

1st SS Panzer Grenadier Regiment Totenkopf
2nd SS Panzer Grenadier Regiment Totenkopf
3rd Panzer Regiment SS Panzer Grenadier
Reconnaissance Battalion
FlaK Battalion (4 batteries)
Panzerjäger (AT) Battalion
Sturmgeschütz Battalion (4 batteries)
Signals Battalion
Pioneer Battalion

Named Panzergrenadier Regiments
1st SS Panzer Grenadier Regiment 'Thule'
3rd SS Panzer Grenadier Regiment 'Theodor Eicke'

Summer 1943
Reconnaissance battalion, additional six companies, and the Panzer Regiment by eight companies.

October 1943
Designation from the Führer as a Panzer Division.
3rd Panzer Division Totenkopf

Panzergrenadier renumbered
5th SS Panzer Grenadier Regiment 'Thule'
6th SS Panzer Grenadier Regiment 'Theodor Eicke'

Totenkopf Commanders 1939–45

Rank	Name	Dates of Service
SS-Obergruppenführer	Theodor Eicke	1 Nov 1939 – 7 Jul 1941
SS-Obergruppenführer	Matthias Kleinheisterkamp	7 Jul 1941 – 18 Jul 1941
SS-Obergruppenführer	Georg Keppler	18 Jul 1941 – 19 Sep 1941
SS-Obergruppenführer	Theodor Eicke	19 Sep 1941 – 26 Feb 1943
SS-Obergruppenführer	Hermann Priess	26 Feb 1943 – 27 Apr 1943
SS-Gruppenführer	Heinz Lammerding	27 Apr 1943 – 15 May 1943
SS-Gruppenführer	Max Simon	15 May 1943 – 22 Oct 1943
SS-Obergruppenführer	Hermann Priess	22 Oct 1943 – 21 Jun 1944
SS-Brigadeführer	Hellmuth Becker	21 Jun 1944 – 8 May 1945

Ranks

German Army	Waffen-SS	British Army equivalent
Gemeiner, Landser	Schütze	Private
	Oberschütze	
Grenadier	Sturmmann	Lance Corporal
Obergrenadier		
Gefreiter	Rottenführer	Corporal
Obergefreiter	Unterscharführer	
Stabsgefreiter		
Unteroffizier	Scharführer	Sergeant
Unterfeldwebel	Oberscharführer	Colour Sergeant

German Army	Waffen-SS	British Army equivalent
Feldwebel		
Oberfeldwebel	Hauptscharführer	Sergeant Major
Stabsfeldwebel	Hauptbereitschaftsleiter	
	Sturmscharführer	Warrant Officer
Leutnant	Unterstumführer	Second Lieutenant
Oberleutnant	Obersturmführer	First Lieutenant
Hauptmann	Hauptsturmführer	Captain
Major	Sturmbannführer	Major
Oberstleutnant	Obersturmbannführer	Lieutenant Colonel
Oberst	Standartenführer	Colonel
	Oberführer	Brigadier General
Generalmajor	Brigadeführer	Major General
Generalleutnant	Gruppenführer	Lieutenant General
General	Obergruppenführer	General
Generaloberst	Oberstgruppenführer	
Generalfeldmarschall	Reichsführer-SS	Field Marshal